THE JOURNEY OF SURVIVAL,HOPE & INTERCONNECTING TIME

SAHILDEEP SINGH RAINA

Copyright © Sahildeep Singh Raina
All Rights Reserved.

TO
1.THE "ALMIGHTY GOD" my biggest inspiration
2.MY GRANDPARENTS who are giving me Blessings from above
3. My biggest strength : MY FAMILY

Contents

Contents

Preface

This book is based on the poetry about life, its trials, the motivation and way out to succeed. And also about bonds of friendship. The role of women, family and our belief in the Almighty too.

Acknowledgements

This is my first experience in Writing. Poetry has always been big passion.

A big thanks to my father "S. Parveen Singh Raina" & my mother "Mrs. Kulbir Kaur Raina" for inculcating positive beliefs in me.

My guide "DR. NEELIKA ARORA" for always being my biggest Source of Inspiration.. My teachers DR. SUVIDHA KHANNA & DR. PALLVI ARORA who have always been there for me when I needed them.

My Wife "MRS. RASMEET KAUR" for understanding me more than I understand myself.

My cute nephew "HRIDAAN SINGH" whose one smile encourages me all the time..

I also want to thank my sister "DR CHANDPREET KAUR" for being my constant motivator

This acknowledgement is incomplete without the mention of two besties "DEVIA NANDA" & "ADITYA SALGOTRA" who are my constant support through THICK & THIN & always motivate me to WIN..

About The Author

SAHILDEEP SINGH RAINA
BORN IN JAMMU CITY, JAMMU & KASHMIR
STUDIED MBA IN TOURISM & PGDCCM From JAMMU
UNIVERSITY.
IS A HUGE BELIEVER OF GOD & BELIEVES THAT GOD
IS ALWAYS THERE FOR THOSE WHO BELIEVE IN HIM.
HAS A HUGE PASSION FOR POETRY WRITING & HAS
POETRY PUBLISHED IN newspaper as well. ☺?☺?

CHAPTER ONE

Ability To Survive

*There are four seasons and for every one of these there are
few reasons.
Everything will get a rise and we will have a surprise.
Some surprises are awesome while some may give us a
shock.
Even when situation gets tough, we must stand strong as a
rock.
Life is a very tough thing to understand.
Some things are small while lot of things are grand.
There is always a sense of being responsible.
When you are being responsible, everything is possible.
Some things have to occur in a resolute as well as absolute
manner.
If not handled well, things will come under the scanner.
Handle the things well and let the opportunities create.
Hard work is always rewarded and good things will
reciprocate.*

CHAPTER TWO

Bringing Out The Best

The almighty's hand us always there.
When this happens, I overcome the instant fear.
The troubleshooting is very instant.
The fear is easy removed, the happiness becomes constant.
This life is like a complete bag of requisition of desires.
It's fine that you are ambitious and fight fire with fire.
The family is then your biggest support.
You may sneak away from everything, but almighty is
make your final report.
Ignore the complexities and bring out the qualities.
The people may degrade you, but never forget your
sensitivities.

CHAPTER THREE

Easy & Tough

Opportunities are sometimes easy to find.
And sometimes they make us grind.
There should be something worthy to give and take.
Otherwise the real things might become fake.
The lines may be cheesy and heart may be clean.
There are few slim fit things and some things are lean.
Learn to go extra mile and take your chance.
When things become good, there is a sense of romance.
There is a big involvement of both truth and dare.
When you want to improve, have some time in spare.
You might be wrong and sometimes you are right.
Have a clear vision and nothing will go out of sight.

CHAPTER FOUR

Friendship Day

A friend is the one who stands by your side.
When he is there, there is nothing to hide.
He is like a one huge bubble.
He is a one big shield who can never see you in trouble.
When a friend is there your sorrows turn to happiness.
The life turns smooth and nothing remains mess.
A friend is always your source of motivation.
When friendship occurs there remains no obligation.
In our lives they have no self-greed.
They give us their own desires to succeed.
God bless the friends who give us a proper stand.
In our toughest times, they give us their own hand.

CHAPTER FIVE

Life & It's Connection

*We know what we become, sometimes good and sometimes
bad.
They can be few shades of grey as well.
On the earth I can see both heaven and hell.
There is existence of both positive as well negative vibes.
And if I am good and gracious enough we won't make any
sarcastic jibes.
The truth of the matter is we have the Almighty's belief.
When things are tough, he gives us sense of relief.
All the good things that come have no hard fast rule.
When good things arrive we take them as a student who is
going to school.
It is therefore good that we are beware and be aware.
Then the bad things will not give us a stare.*

CHAPTER SIX

The Journeys

Life is a journey, sometimes good, sometimes bad.
Even when we are at loggerheads, we cannot remain sad.
When life is rough, we need to be tough.
When there is toughness, there will be no mess.
We always give our hundred per cent.
There is a sense of self-esteem; responsibility never gives
you a dent.
There is always some fire that is always exciting.
Sometimes it is small; sometimes it is a big thing.
Life does take some serious turn.
When you work on your aspirations, you will surely
deserve and earn.
When there is prosperity, there is no disparity.
The life may give you trouble; still there is no need to live in
small bubble.

CHAPTER SEVEN

The Almighty's World

The Almighty is the one who we trust.
With all the positive vibes, we overcome all our rust.
There is a feeling of goodness in all the sense.
Everything is cleared and nothing remains dense.
There exists the feeling of belongingness.
Things change for better and nothing remains a mess.
The world is messy and very complicated.
Among all the rough roads, a smooth way is thereby
created.
With the blessings of Almighty there exists a big-time
hope.
And he only gives us the power, that we tightly held it with
rope.

CHAPTER EIGHT

Opportunities To Life

There is always something special about life.
Sometimes it is simple; sometimes it is a double-edged
knife.
We need to put up a good fight.
Sometimes we might be wrong, sometimes we are right.
We are many times handed over the charge.
Sometimes the tasks are small, sometimes they are large.
There is a need of in-built strength.
It can help us go to any length.
Wonderful things are there to give us a chance.
Make the best of them because it is like requisite romance.

CHAPTER NINE

The Corrections & Better Things

There are few things that are very tough to get.
We cry big time, our eyes become wet.
We are enquired about good, ugly and bad.
The life becomes tough, we might become sad.
There are few we want to achieve.
Many a times we only selectively perceive.
The selective perception can be barrier.
It becomes an unnecessary load carrier.
This load carrier needs to be erected.
There will be many things which will therefore be corrected.

CHAPTER TEN

The Desire To Improve

There is always something in our hearts that is hidden.
When we are not able to express, it makes us guilt-ridden.
The desperation is shown right on our face.
The counting time starts, we only give the chase.
Our heart is sometimes strong and sometimes it is frail.
When it goes off the track, it will derail.
The troubles that throng us will move away.
It will happen if we keep our sorrows at bay.
There is a hidden courage that keeps us zooming.
It ultimately helps in our better grooming.

CHAPTER ELEVEN

Willingness To Survive

The trait of leader always resides within.
You need to be good and don't have to commit a sin.
The troubles can only give u a single trouble.
But when you are positive towards life, the happiness will double.
There is always going to be the desperate time that is never sold.
Only your times are new, the trials might be old.
With all the good things, the tough things never cross our path.
The result is simple and we will never bear anybody's wrath.
Make some effort and then work hard.
Things might get tough but do make it your own yard.

CHAPTER TWELVE

Being Yourself

There may be few things that are unavailable.
Few things are in a mess while few things are stable.
Why become a monk and remain in a hermit?
The life gets a chance with many things in permit.
You are always seeker for best.
Be rational and thoughtful and there is no test.
Everything is fine when your mind and heart will combine.
Think positive and always shine like a star.
Remain motivated and grounded, the success is not far.

The Survival & Our Belief

The desire to learn is like a strong wall.
The result is that among the storm, we can stand tall.
There is an in-built capacity that helps us immense.
Everything gets cleared which is very dense.
The timing may be different but time is always right.
And nothing tends to get out of the sight.
The line gets clear when you know what is exact.
There will be difference between fiction and fact.
Have faith in almighty and keep the belief.
When the things get better, there is always sense of belief.

The Real Test

It is a mad, mad world.
We all need some space.
When the competition has also started for us.
This is when we start our race.
This race is sometimes hard and sometimes fast.
It will continue to happen, as long as we last.
Survival is the key, when the times are hard.
It is when we push that extra yard.
This extra yard is test of our ability.
This is when we show our capability.

The Morals

Sometimes with life we have direct contact.
That is why we keep things intact.
Nothing is permanent, but few things do matter.
Nothing is easy, that comes to us on a platter.
After morning comes afternoon.
Not everyone is born with a silver spoon.
Keep trying and look for the chance which is ultimate.
Even when chances are not there, make them create.
You create everything on your own.
When hard work is harvested well, its rich seeds are sown.

CHAPTER SIXTEEN

The Story Our Times

There is a story; our life has made us told.
Few of the chapters are new, while few chapters are old.
There is a new story, which will rise.
Few lines are very cheap, while few have a high price.
The stakes are high, which we will share.
Sometimes there are truth, sometimes there is dare.
The things will definitely change for permanent.
This is when we give our hundred per cent.
The sun that will set will also shine and rise.
This is when story reaches its climax and our
opportunities arise.

CHAPTER SEVENTEEN

The Desire To Succeed

There are few drops of water, few pieces of Ice.
Sometimes the world is cruel; you still have to be nice.
There is big crossover between being good and bad.
Failures do exist, but they cannot make us sad.
Time sometimes makes us its slave.
But we have to turn the tide and control the wave.
Few drops of Ice are in pieces and bit.
Our amazing transformation will make us shine and lit.
There are demerits, there can be a barrier.
When opportunities cease to come, we have to become its carrier.
Few drops of water are up in the sky.
Keep the ambitions up, keep the motivation high

The Times Of Life

The experiences teach us to be great and better.
Being Courageous is such a wonderful letter.
You get lost in time and strive for success.
But nothing should go ahead in excess.
We should be confident and properly trained.
It is essential that we don't get emotionally drained.
Sometimes things are good, sometimes on wrong side.
It is essential we pick up the right tide.
No times are easy and plans become extempore.
It is therefore essential we know everything to the core.

CHAPTER NINETEEN

The Reality

The world and us is sometimes dissimilar and sometimes same.
The patterns are different, just like a cat-mouse game.
We want to survive; perfection is always we always thrive.
Hoping for the better things, the bad omen hopefully never stings.
The reality is crude, sometimes happy, and sometimes rude.
But we always thrive for excellence, especially in the proper sense.
The job is to win and strive big.
And ignore those who are taking your dig.
The reality of life is to get better and strong
That's where you will always last really long.

The World & Us

Welcome to this world, where you always belong.
To survive the competition, you have to get along.
Life is never easy and we should always try.
And we are not losers who will begin to cry.
The trials and tribulations though many may cause us to broke.
But amidst all situations we have to remain a tough bloke.
This world may be tough, whose one side may be slightly rough.
But we cannot bog down and should get the victory crown.
Have faith, remain calm and remain contented.
This will help you to get what you have intended.

CHAPTER TWENTY-ONE

CHAPTER TWENTY-TWO

Family: A Gift Forever

When there is family, there is assurance.
This is the time, you need no insurance.
They give you shelter, they stand by your side.
And make your horrendous ride to a joyful ride.
The family time is there forever.
This is the time that we forget never.
Life is easy with family and their care.
It's our biggest truth, especially when there is any dare.
When we are down and out, we always need a lift.
Our family to us is the God's biggest gift.

When There Are You

Between you and me, there is nothing to hide.
When you stand by me, no ride is a bumpy ride.
I will take your stand; will take your hand in my hand.
It's only you and me who really are there.
All I need then is your love and care.
I know to me it is you who belong.
When life is not smooth, your presence will make me get along.
You are my star, you are my light.
When there is darkness, you always keep it bright.
What I love most is your million-dollar smile.
For this I can even go a mile.

CHAPTER TWENTY-FOUR

Girl Child: Her Life & Time

What if she is a girl, she also has a life.
She is somebody's daughter, she is somebody's wife.
There is a life that belongs to her only.
When she is in trouble, don't keep her lonely.
The life is different and involves a new turn.
The respect is what she wants to earn.
Life is equal for all, be it big or small.
The girl wants respect;
She doesn't want that her closed ones suspect.
The girl child is no longer a burden.
She brings a family together and spreads the fragrance
that never ends.

CHAPTER TWENTY-FIVE

Raksha Bandhan : A True Bond

There is a bond of love; there is a bond of care.
This is the bond that a brother – sister share.
There exists a proper bond of trust.
No matter how old we grow this bond will never rust.
Brother and sister are like shadows to no end.
Their relation is that curve that will never bend.
Raksha Bandhan is a festival of being together and
relation that is strong.
The bond between brother and sister always lasts long.
There is prayer of safety, well-being and belongingness.
No matter how far a brother and sister are, this bond
always brings togetherness.